KT-482-732

DINOSAUR WORLD

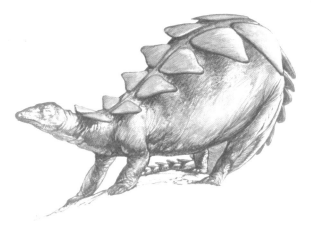

A Piccolo Factbook

Contents

DINOSAUR WORLD

By David Lambert

Editor: Jacqui Bailey

Series Design: David Jefferis

A Piccolo Factbook

Before the Dinosaurs

Dinosaurs included the largest and most terrifying animals that ever lived on land. For scores of millions of years they ruled the world, then suddenly died out. To find out how they began we must first see how life itself began and changed.

More than 4000 million years ago the world was very hot. Smoke and molten rock spurted from volcanoes. Steam and gases hung above the land and water. Storms raged. As the world cooled down, torrents of rain filled the oceans. There were no living things.

But in the oceans life was being brewed. Energy from sunshine and lightning joined chemical substances to make the tiny building blocks for life. The first living things built from these substances may have been bacteria. These little organisms gobbled up ready-made food substances in the water faster than they were being formed. Then one organism gained the knack of taking in energy from sunlight to make its own food from simple substances in the air or water. Such organisms gave rise to green plants. Once there were green plants there could be animals, for all animals eat plants or other animals.

Life in the Early Oceans

Living things were swimming in the oceans more than 3000 million years ago. Each early bacterium and the first plants were made of just one tiny package called a *cell*. These cells are so small that a quarter of a million bacteria could fit on this full stop. Once a bacterium cell has reached a certain size it splits in two, making two new bacteria. If the parent cell tries to go on growing instead of splitting it might die. For once a cell grows beyond a certain size it cannot do the jobs that must be done to stay alive—jobs like taking in enough food and oxygen to power the cell, and getting rid of wastes.

Many Cells that Work as One

When cells clump together and divide their work between them, they can form far larger living things. In fact the tallest tree and largest whale are built up from millions of cells so small that you would need a microscope to see them clearly.

The first colonies of living cells swam or clung to the sea bed 1000 million years ago or more. Most of these simple plants and animals produced young ones like themselves. But some young ones were not exactly like their parents, and their children were slightly different again. In this way

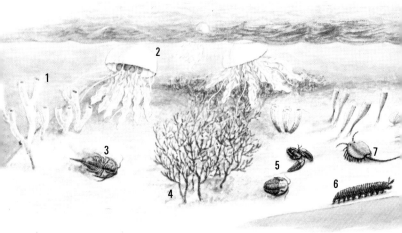

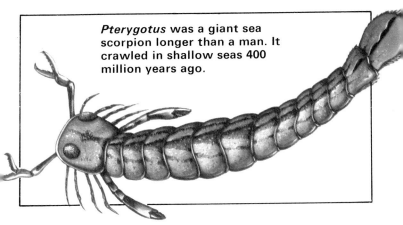

Pterygotus was a giant sea scorpion longer than a man. It crawled in shallow seas 400 million years ago.

many thousand kinds of living things appeared. Those best at finding food and avoiding being eaten multiplied. But other kinds died out.

By 500 million years ago the sea already held plants and creatures much like some still living today.

Below: Some of the earliest living things, 600–500 million years ago. 1 sponges; 2 jellyfish; 3, 5, 14, 15 trilobites; 4 red algae; 6 *Aysheia*; 7 *Burgessia*; 8, 16 lamp shells; 9 *Emeraldella*; 10 corals; 11 *Waptia*; 12 *Marrella*; 13 green algae; 17 sea lilies; 18 echinoderms; 19 ragworm.

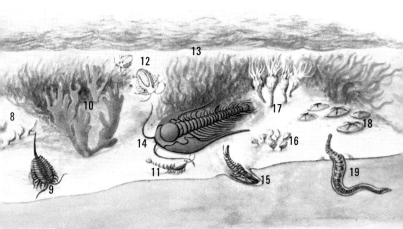

The First Fishes

Among the sea creatures of long ago, there was one whose descendants would give rise to the dinosaurs.

Impossible Monsters

Certain sea beasts could never have given rise to big land animals. For instance there were such soft-bodied creatures as the jellyfish. A jellyfish washed up on the shore cannot lift itself or move about on land.

Jointed-legged creatures like crabs and trilobites could walk on land. But their bodies were given strength and protection by a shell, an outside skeleton. Most such creatures have to shed this as they get bigger, and then grow a new one. Before the new shell hardens the animal is soft. During the period when it had shed its shell a big land animal would not have been able to move about to find food or escape its enemies. So the jointed-legged animals did not give rise to dinosaurs either.

Building with Bone

The dinosaurs' ancestor was a soft-bodied creature with a difference. That creature may have been related to the sea squirts of today. Unlike jellyfish, young sea squirts are strengthened by a stiff rod running through the tail, called a *notochord*.

Stiffeners like this later gave rise to backbones. A backbone is a strong bony rod made up of many joints. Creatures strengthened by a backbone and a skeleton of other bones inside their body do not have to shed their skeleton as they grow.

The Age of Fishes

The first backboned animals were fishes. Fishes were swimming in the sea by 500 million years ago. But they became plentiful in the so-called Age of Fishes, from 395–345 million years ago.

Dinichthys was a placoderm more than 9 metres long. This formidable monster's jagged jaws could crush the armour of the early, jawless fishes.

Four Kinds of Fishes

The first fishes were small creatures without jaws. Their mouths were simply holes. These fishes sucked in particles of food with water as they grubbed about in the mud. Some had bony heads. Others had bodies guarded by thick scales. Early jawless fishes are called ostracoderms or 'shell skins'. Certain jawless fishes gave rise to fishes with jaws that could be shut and opened. Among these were the placoderms, protected by an armoured head. Some placoderms had jaws strong enough to crunch through other fishes' armour. A third group of fishes were sharks and rays—fishes with soft cartilage instead of bone. Fourth were the bony fishes, which we shall come to later.

The First Land Plants

While fishes were evolving in the seas, plants began to gain a hold upon the land. Land plants helped to make it possible for animals to follow them ashore. For all creatures depend on plants for their food.

The land had two advantages for plants which they did not have in water. One was brighter sunshine to help them make their food. The other was more oxygen—the gas that living things breathe. But there were snags as well.

Early plants like seaweeds were suited to life in the water. They made food and kept moist just by taking substances from the water all around them. Water also helped to hold them up. A seaweed washed ashore soon dies. It lacks a stem stiff enough to hold it up. It lacks roots to draw up moisture and nourishment from soil. Its leaf-like upper parts are not waterproof, so they quickly shrivel and dry up in the open air.

Plant Pioneers

The first plants to leave the water may have been related to the tiny algal plants that form green scum in ponds. By 400 million years ago certain algae had given rise to plants better shaped for life on land. *Cooksonia* (below) was just a cluster of stems without true roots. Other early land plants included clubmosses very similar to those alive today. Later came the ferns and horsetails. These were land plants with roots to suck up minerals and water. Their stiff stems held the leaves up to the light. Tubes inside the stems took water to the leaves and brought food to the roots. The leaves had a waxy 'skin' to stop the moisture leaking out. Some clubmosses and horsetails grew into tall trees. The Age of Fishes was also the Age of the First Forests.

The First Land Animals

Many kinds of creature evolved in the early oceans. But very few gave rise to animals able to take up life upon the land. The pioneers probably came from the invertebrates (animals without a backbone). By 370 million years ago three groups had made their home on land. These groups were some worms, some molluscs (soft-bodied animals including snails and slugs), and some arthropods (jointed-legged animals like spiders, crabs, and insects). However, worms and slugs soon die if their soft, moist bodies are exposed to air, but arthropods are different.

Scavengers like this cockroach (above) and hunters like this scorpion (below) lived on the floors of warm, wet forests more than 300 million years ago.

Insects, Spiders and their Kin

The arthropods' soft, moist insides are safe inside a waterproof case. Then too, their strong, jointed legs allowed certain arthropods to walk in open air without the help of water to support their bodies. Many arthropods gained ways of breathing dry air without drying up their moist insides. Insects, for instance, have tiny air holes in their outer skeleton. Air flows through these holes to all parts of the body.

Browsers and Hunters

The first arthropods on land may have been the ancestors of the many-legged creatures we call millipedes, which feed on dead and rotting plants. Soon there were hunters too: beasts like centipedes, scorpions and spiders. Insects became by far the most plentiful land animals. But successful though they were, arthropods still had to shed their protective cases as they grew. This meant that they could not grow very large on land.

A hard waterproof case kept moist the insides of creatures like this centipede and millipede.

From Fins to Legs

Earlier we mentioned the rise of bony fishes in the Age of Fishes. These creatures were the ancestors of dinosaurs and all the other backboned animals that have ever lived on land. Most bony fishes have bony rays to support their fins. But another group, the bony lobe-finned fishes, had fins that grew from fleshy stubs jutting from the body like stumpy limbs. These were the first fishes to move ashore. In time such lobes gave rise to the legs of all backboned land animals.

Three Groups of Lobe-Fins

More than 345 million years ago there lived three groups of lobe-fins. Coelacanths had strong stumpy fins but could not have breathed on land. Those living nowadays swim in the sea. Lungfish had bags that worked as lungs. When their pools dried up, prehistoric lungfish burrowed in the mud and breathed ordinary air, as living lungfish do today.

The third group of lobe-fins were the rhipidistians. None is still alive today. But in the Age of Fishes there were plenty of these flesh-eaters. They grew up to three metres long. Like coelacanths they had strong, stumpy fins. Like lungfish they had lungs. Some swam in salty seas, but others lived entirely in fresh water.

One freshwater kind was *Eusthenopteron*. The bones of its paired fins probably gave rise to the leg bones of backboned land animals. Like them, *Eusthenopteron* had an airway joining the roof of its mouth and its nostrils.

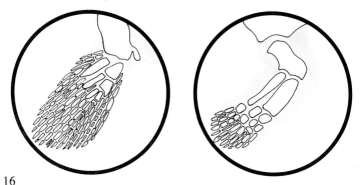

If its pool dried up, this fish could walk to another. If a big fish chased baby *Eusthenopterons* they could scamper ashore for safety. They may have learned to stay to feed on insects.

So a fish began to spend part of its life on the banks of pools and rivers. Backboned animals had begun their invasion of dry land.

Above: *Eusthenopteron* seizing another fish. Young *Eusthenopterons* may have first gone ashore to escape their own parents' jaws.

Below, from left to right: Changes that must have taken place for a lobed fin to give rise to an amphibian's leg shaped to walk on land.

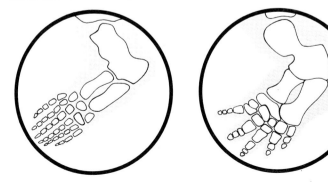

Amphibians Arrive

On dry land, lobe-finned fishes such as *Eusthenopteron* levered themselves awkwardly along upon their stumpy fins. But by 350 million years ago they had given rise to a group of backboned creatures that were more at home on land. These creatures were amphibians—prehistoric relatives of our living frogs and salamanders.

The First Amphibians

The first known amphibian was *Ichthyostega*. This squat, sprawling beast measured about a metre. Its tail and the roof bones of its skull were much like those of the lobe-finned fish it came from. The main difference was in its limbs. Instead of paired fins, it had four legs, with five toes on each foot. Its leg bones were strong enough to bear its weight and its leg muscles were powerful enough for walking.

The Swamp Dwellers

Ichthyostega or beasts much like it gave rise to a whole zoo of amphibians. They lived in the hot swampy forests that covered huge low areas of land around 300 million years ago.

Many kinds belonged to a group of amphibians called lepospondyls. These tended to be weak, skinny creatures. Some lost their legs and swam like water snakes. Others had small, weak limbs.

Most of the prehistoric amphibians were labyrinthodonts or 'labyrinth teeth'. Labyrinthodonts got their name from their hollow teeth whose complicated walls reminded scientists of some kind of maze or labyrinth.

Some big labyrinthodonts had sharp, strong teeth and hunted at least partly on dry land.

Such beasts were better built for life on land than the first amphibians. They had stronger bones to bear their body weight. They had eardrums that could pick up sounds travelling through air. Airborne sounds are much fainter than sounds that travel through water. The later amphibians also had eyelids that helped to keep their eyes moist when they were out of water.

Prisoners of Water

Amphibians still needed the water. Many had to bathe to stop their moist skins drying up. Their eggs had no waterproof shell, so they were laid in water. Amphibians did not live all their lives on land. But they gave rise to backboned animals that did.

Lepospondyl amphibians living 300 million years ago:
Phlegethontia (left);
Ophiderpeton (centre);
Microbrachis (right).

A battle between two flesh-eating reptiles of about 270 million years ago. *Dimetrodon* (with a sail-like 'radiator') bites *Ophiacodon's* neck.

The First Reptiles

About 290 million years ago amphibians gave rise to reptiles. These creatures could live entirely on dry land.

The first reptiles were small, low-slung beasts that looked much like amphibians. But they were different in important ways. First, they had a scaly, waterproof skin. Second, their eggs had a tough or hard shell that was also waterproof. So reptiles did not have to lay their eggs in water to prevent their drying up. Third, reptiles had leg bones that made it possible for them to run instead of wriggling along as salamanders do. Lastly their improved blood supply and breathing system helped provide them with the energy to run.

Reptiles Multiply

As deserts took the place of swampy forests, amphibians grew scarcer, but the reptiles multiplied. By 250 million years ago, reptiles came in many shapes and sizes. Blunt-toothed kinds ate plants. Sharp-toothed kinds ate flesh.

Right: *Dimetrodon* babies hatching from their eggs. While amphibians lay soft, jelly-like eggs, the reptiles lay eggs with a tough or hard waterproof shell. Such shells hold stores of food and water. They help to prevent the unhatched young from drying up.

'Terrible Lizards'

By 205 million years ago, reptiles had given rise to dinosaurs. Their name means 'terrible lizards'. The remains of these huge prehistoric beasts do indeed look like lizards. But many experts believe that the dinosaurs were not cold-blooded reptiles, but warm-blooded as birds and mammals are.

Some were four-legged giants bigger than a bus; others, two-legged dwarfs no larger than a goose. There were fierce flesh-eaters and docile plant-eaters. Early kinds gave rise to others that took their place. For 140 million years dinosaurs were masters of the land.

How Dinosaurs Began

The first dinosaurs came from swimming reptiles. These ancestors hunted their prey in water. Their strong, flattened tail helped them to swim, and their long, back legs could thrust down and back to push them forward. From such beasts came *Euparkeria* a reptile like a small, long-legged crocodile. *Euparkeria* lived on land. It walked on all four legs but ran on its hind legs.

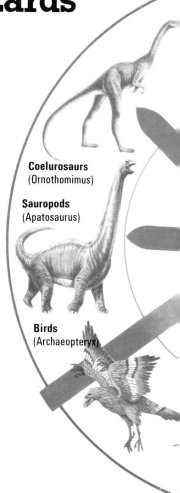

Coelurosaurs
(Ornothomimus)

Sauropods
(Apatosaurus)

Birds
(Archaeopteryx)

Euparkeria and its kin probably gave rise to both the two main groups of dinosaur. These are called the bird-hipped dinosaurs and the lizard-hipped dinosaurs,

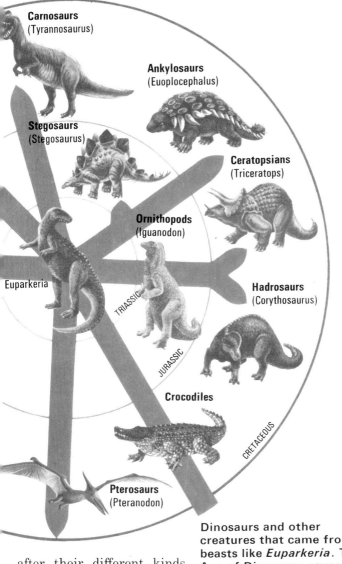

Carnosaurs
(Tyrannosaurus)

Ankylosaurs
(Euoplocephalus)

Stegosaurs
(Stegosaurus)

Ceratopsians
(Triceratops)

Ornithopods
(Iguanodon)

Euparkeria

TRIASSIC

Hadrosaurs
(Corythosaurus)

JURASSIC

Crocodiles

CRETACEOUS

Pterosaurs
(Pteranodon)

after their different kinds of hip bones. In this chapter we look at the amazing lizard-hipped dinosaurs.

Dinosaurs and other creatures that came from beasts like *Euparkeria*. The Age of Dinosaurs covered the Triassic, Jurassic, and Cretaceous periods of Earth history.

23

Apatosaurus was once called *Brontosaurus*, or 'thunder lizard'. The man who named it supposed this giant's feet thumped the ground with sounds like thunder as it walked along.

The Giants

Among the lizard-hipped dinosaurs were the largest animals that ever lived on land. Scientists call these giants sauropods or 'lizard-footed' dinosaurs. Each monster had a huge, barrel-shaped body, four legs like tree trunks, a long neck with a small head, and a long tail that tapered to a point. The largest sauropods may have weighed more than the heaviest whales alive today, and perhaps stood taller than a building seven storeys high.

Despite their massive size and strength sauropods were gentle giants. They ate plants growing in the warm forests that covered many lands 200 million years ago.

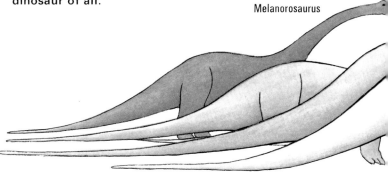

Five sauropods compared for size. *Brachiosaurus* was the largest of the five. *Diplodocus* was the longest dinosaur of all.

Melanorosaurus

A World of Monsters

The giant dinosaurs multiplied, and many kinds spread far across the world. All the sauropods probably sprang from *Ticinosuchus*. This reptile relative of *Euparkeria* walked on all fours and measured 3 metres in length.

By 200 million years ago *Ticinosuchus* had given rise to sauropods like *Melanorosaurus* which was as long as seven men laid end to end. Later sauropods were larger still. *Cetiosaurus* ('whale lizard') grew up to half as long again as *Melanorosaurus*. *Apatosaurus* (also called *Brontosaurus*) grew as long as 14 men laid end to end.

The Supergiants

The longest-ever land animal was *Diplodocus* or 'double beam', called after the shape of a type of bone found in its tail. *Diplodocus* grew up to 27 metres long. But *Diplodocus* was much lighter than *Brachiosaurus* ('arm lizard'). *Brachiosaurus* was so named because its front legs were longer than most sauropods'. This giant weighed as much as 20 elephants. In 1972, American bone-hunters found remains of an even mightier monster in Colorado. Nicknamed *Supersaurus*, this unbelievable creature may have weighed as much as 50 large elephants.

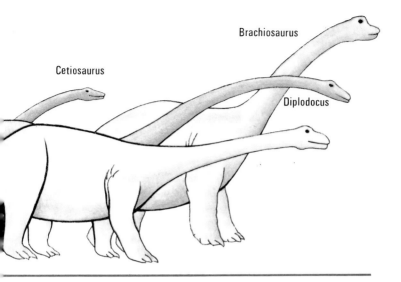

Brachiosaurus

Cetiosaurus

Diplodocus

Living Factories to Process Food

Being big may have helped the sauropods to stay alive. When air cools down at night, large cold-blooded animals lose body heat more slowly than small ones. If sauropods were cold-blooded, their large size would have helped to keep their bodies warm and active. Then, too, if flesh-eating dinosaurs attacked them they were big enough to crush and kill all but their largest, fiercest enemies.

Maybe the sauropods needed to be big to digest enough plant food to keep their bodies working. Their peg-like teeth were poor at grinding leaves. This work had to be done mainly in the stomach, where swallowed pebbles may have worked like millstones to crush the leaves to pulp. So a sauropod probably needed an extra-large stomach. If so, it also needed a large body to contain that stomach.

How they Lived

Sauropods used their long necks like giraffes to help them browse among the tree-tops. Some ate half a tonne of leaves a day. Like today's elephants they roamed in herds. This helped protect them from their enemies. The Sun's heat hatched the eggs they laid, but we do not know if the parents stayed to guard their babies.

An *Allosaurus* (right) chases a *Coelurus* (left) in North America 150 million years ago. Big plant-eating dinosaurs browse in the distance.

Two-legged Hunters

While the huge sauropods munched they no doubt kept alert to danger. Their greatest threat came from the theropods or 'beast feet'. There were two groups of these two-legged hunters.

Bird-like Beasts

One group of theropods was made up of dinosaurs that looked surprisingly like birds. They had a slim body, and long legs, neck and tail.

They also had teeth; arms with claws not wings; and scales, not feathers.

These bird-like dinosaurs are known as coelurosaurs, after *Coelurus*. This beast was longer than a man but lighter. It ran quickly on its long hind legs, with its neck stretched out ahead and balanced by its tail.

Coelurus probably darted into bushes after lizards and small mammals. It may even have captured birds.

Frightful Fangs

The real danger to big browsing dinosaurs came not from coelurosaurs but from larger theropods: the carnosaurs.

Among the early carnosaurs none was more terrible than *Allosaurus* ('leaping lizard'). Allosaurus was 12 metres long. It walked on two huge hind legs, armed with sharp claws. The front legs were short. But a thick neck supported a large head that had mighty jaws bristling with teeth like knives. *Allosaurus* preyed upon the sauropods of North America about 150 million years ago.

The Tyrant King

The largest and most terrifying of the carnosaurs were the tyrannosaurs or 'tyrant lizards'. These lived late on in the Age of Dinosaurs. The best-known of them all is *Tyrannosaurus rex*: 'king of the tyrant lizards'. *Tyrannosaurus* was alive and killing even larger dinosaurs in North America about 70 million years ago.

A Killer's Weapons

At 14 metres long, *Tyrannosaurus* could have reared high enough to peer into upstairs windows if there had been any. It was heavier than most elephants, and each powerful

Tyrannosaurus ate the plant-eating dinosaurs. Many had no defence against its mighty jaws.

hind leg bore a load heavier than a large rhinoceros. The hind toes had claws like carving knives. Fangs as long as a man's hand lined the massive jaws in a skull with eye sockets each larger than your head.

Strangely, *Tyrannosaurus*'s arms were tiny: too small for weapons; too short to bring food to its mouth.

An *Ornithomimus* keeps watch for enemies as it raids a clutch of eggs laid by another dinosaur.

Ostrich Dinosaurs

Struthiomimus was an ostrich dinosaur that may also have stolen eggs laid in the sand. Such big, bird-like beasts could have used their hands to scoop away the sand. Their claws may have helped to smash the eggs open.

Late in the Age of Dinosaurs lived the largest of the bird-like coelurosaurs. These creatures looked something like a plucked ostrich with long legs and a long tail. But they also had arms with claw-tipped 'hands'. Light, hollow bones made up the skeleton, and their jaws were just toothless beaks.

Champion Sprinters
Big bird-like coelurosaurs may have used their hands to gather fruit or shellfish, tear open ants' nests, or steal other dinosaurs' eggs.

If an enemy came near, an ostrich dinosaur made off at speed. It could probably run as fast as an ostrich—about 80 km/h. Only warm-blooded creatures can reach that speed. So it seems extremely likely that these big bird-like dinosaurs were not cold-blooded reptiles.

Bird-hipped Dinosaurs

The largest and fiercest dinosaurs both belonged to the lizard-hipped group. But many bird-hipped dinosaurs were also very large, and some were even stranger than their relatives. All bird-hipped dinosaurs ate plants. Some walked on two legs, but others went about on all fours.

One of the first bird-hipped dinosaurs was *Fabrosaurus*. No bigger than a large lizard, *Fabrosaurus* stood on long hind legs, like a flesh-eating dinosaur. But its horny beak and grinding teeth were clearly made for cropping and munching leaves. It lived in southern Africa.

Bird-footed Dinosaurs

Fabrosaurus gave rise to much bigger ornithopods, or 'bird-footed' dinosaurs. Among the largest was *Iguanodon*. *Iguanodon* was named after its teeth, which resembled those of modern iguana lizards. The creature was as heavy as an elephant, but less well armed. *Iguanodon* had only sharp spikes on its thumbs to protect it against attack.

An *Iguanodon* grunts with pain as a megalosaur lunges at its thigh. The *Iguanodon* may stab its sharp thumbs at its enemy's eyes to make it break off the attack.

Duck-billed Dinosaurs

As the Age of Dinosaurs drew toward its end, strange relatives of *Iguanodon* multiplied in northern lands. They are called hadrosaurs ('big lizards'). At 9 metres long, hadrosaurs were about as long as *Iguanodon*, but rather less heavy. They walked on big, three-toed hind legs, balanced by a long, heavy tail flattened from side to side. Each arm had four webbed fingers.

Heads with Beaks

The strangest thing about a hadrosaur was the head. This was long, with flat wide jaws that may have had a horny sheath. The jaws were armed with hundreds of teeth. Some kinds of hadrosaur had as many as 2000 teeth, all designed to grind up leaves.

Their duck-like jaws earned hadrosaurs the nickname 'duck-billed dinosaurs'. People used to think they lived like ducks, swimming in lakes or rivers and browsing on soft water plants. Their flattened tails and webbed fingers would certainly have helped them to swim.

But inside the remains of one hadrosaur, scientists found clues to its true way of life. These clues were bits and pieces of what had once been twigs, leaves, fruits and seeds. The hadrosaur had been browsing not on waterweed but on trees.

Duckbills had lived on land. They used their beaks to crop the tough leaves of coniferous trees. Then they mashed these up with their many hundred cheek teeth.

Mysterious Crests

Even stranger than the duckbills' beaks were the bony crests that sprouted from their skulls. Different kinds had different crests. *Kritosaurus* had a ridge above its nose. *Parasaurolophus* had a horn curving backwards from the top of the head. *Corythosaurus* had a tall, rounded crest like a helmet, flattened from side to side.

Experts have many explanations for these crests. The likeliest idea is that they helped the hadrosaurs to recognize their own kind.

Duck-billed dinosaurs of the kind now known as *Parasaurolophus* browse on forest trees. They watch for danger and run away if threatened.

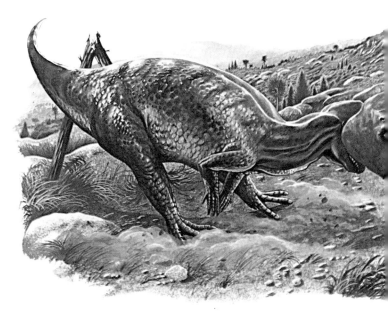

Bone-headed Dinosaurs

At first glance bone-headed dinosaurs seemed far less strange than the duckbills we have been describing. Their heads lacked the duckbills' crests. Yet they were most unusual in another way. Bone-headed dinosaurs get their name because their skulls were so immensely thick.

We can see such skulls in the making if we look at the bony remains of *Yaverlandia*. This bird-hipped, bird-footed dinosaur had two thick bony areas just above the eyes. *Yaverlandia* was no larger than a turkey, and walked carrying its long tail stiffly behind it. *Yaverlandia* gave rise to bigger bone-heads with far thicker skulls.

Bone-heads Large and Small

By the time duck-billed dinosaurs were roaming northern lands so too were animals like the man-sized *Stegoceras*. This creature had a brain no bigger than a hen's egg. Yet that brain lay inside a bony dome up to five times thicker than a human skull.

Much larger and more complicated than this dome was the skull belonging to another bone-head, *Pachycephalosaurus*, meaning 'thick-headed reptile'. The biggest bone-head of them all, this dinosaur protected its small brain inside a skull more than 20 times thicker than a man's, and three times as long as *Stegoceras*'s. Bony spikes jutted upward from the nose, and bony knobs strengthened the thick skull from behind.

Built-in Crash Helmets

Long after people first found the remains of bone-heads their thick skulls remained a mystery. Some scientists suggested that their bones had suffered from disease. Nowadays most experts think that the thick bone saved the creatures' brains from injury when two males banged their heads together in a fight to settle who should win a mate or lead a bone-head herd.

The picture on these pages shows a duel fought between two male *Pachycephalosaurus* dinosaurs. They probably did not fight to kill. The shock as head met head would have simply jarred their backbones.

Plated Dinosaurs

If a fierce flesh-eating dinosaur attacked a bird-hipped dinosaur that walked on its two hind legs, it may have tried to run away. Dinosaurs with long hind legs could probably outpace those that hunted them.

But there was no such escape for the bird-hipped dinosaurs that walked on all fours. Their legs were just too short for sprinting. Instead most must have stood their ground and hoped that their built-in armour would discourage an attack.

Giants in Armour

Some had bony plates to protect parts of the body. Some were all but covered in living armour. Others sprouted massive horns and frills.

The first group to evolve are known now as the stegosaurs, meaning 'plated reptiles'. The earliest known stegosaur was a low-slung animal as long as a car and higher at the hips than at the shoulders. It had a small head with weak jaws, but strong legs and broad feet. Rows of bony bumps along its back offered some defence against attack. Called *Scelidosaurus*, this dinosaur lived in southern England 190 million years ago.

Stegosaurus

From beasts like *Scelidosaurus* sprang *Stegosaurus* – a much larger and better armoured dinosaur. At 9 metres long, *Stegosaurus* was nearly double the length of *Scelidosaurus*, and its back was taller than a man. The beast's hind legs were as massive as an elephant's.

Its main defences were two rows of broad, pointed, bony plates poking up from its back. Some were about a metre long. Two pairs of heavy, curved spikes jutted sideways from the tail to guard it. This dinosaur had a small head and a brain no larger than a walnut.

Stegosaurus roamed northern lands 150 million years ago. Its plates may not have saved it from the carnosaurs, for it died out. But dinosaurs with even heavier armour were to follow.

Plates on *Stegosaurus*'s back may have served as radiators that leaked heat to cool its body. To warm up at dawn, it could have stood so they caught heat from the Sun.

Living Tanks

Plated dinosaurs probably died out because flesh-eaters' claws and fangs sometimes pierced the gaps in their bony defences.

But while the plated dinosaurs were disappearing, much more completely armoured dinosaurs began to multiply. These creatures were the ankylosaurs or 'rounded reptiles', named after their strongly curved ribs. Ankylosaurs tended to be long, low creatures with bony plates, spikes, or knobs protecting most of the parts of the body open to attack.

Early Ankylosaurs
Two kinds of early ankylosaur were roaming southern England before the plated dinosaurs became extinct. One of the newcomers was *Acanthopholis*, a beast about 4 metres long. Flat bony plates ran down its back and tail. The plates were hinged to let it bend its back. Short spines probably protected the back of its neck.

Another early ankylosaur in England was *Polacanthus*. This was somewhat longer than *Acanthopholis* and depended more heavily on spikes for its defence. Rows of tall, bony spikes jutted upward from its head to half-way down its back. Its hips were guarded by a bony shield and a crest of bony triangles ran down its tail.

Later Ankylosaurs
Well protected though they were, the early ankylosaurs were followed by beasts with even better armour.

Above: The tank-like dinosaur *Euoplocephalus* compared with a car to give an idea of its size. Below: the beast looked like this. Carnosaurs may have had their teeth snapped off if they bit into its tough armoured hide.

The whole group takes its name from one of these, once called *Ankylosaurus*, but now renamed *Euoplocephalus*. This North American monster was twice as heavy as *Stegosaurus*, yet only half as long. Sharp-edged plates protected the top of its head, neck, back and a tail that ended in a bony club.

Scolosaurus ('thorn reptile') was even harder to attack. As it shuffled along, the bony plates and sharp spikes covering its top and sides made *Scolosaurus* look like a huge, spiky tortoise.

A Long-lived Group

Only an ankylosaur's belly was soft and vulnerable. But few beasts could overturn one of these low-slung giants to reach its belly. So ankylosaurs lived until the Age of Dinosaurs ended.

Horned Dinosaurs

When carnosaurs attacked the armoured dinosaurs most of them just stood or crouched or swished their heavy tails. But other dinosaurs attacked back with formidable horns that sprouted from their heads. They were the horned dinosaurs.

The Parrot Reptile

Horned dinosaurs had as their ancestor a two-legged dinosaur like *Psittacosaurus* whose name means 'parrot lizard'. The creature's parrot-like beak was probably good at chopping off the tough leaves of flowering plants. These were new kinds of plant that spread from Mongolia, where *Psittacosaurus* lived 100 million years ago.

This man-sized dinosaur probably gave rise to *Protoceratops* ('first horned face'). *Protoceratops* walked on all fours and weighed more than 1.5 tonnes. A big bony frill at the back of its skull formed an anchor for its powerful jaw muscles.

Horns and Frills

From *Protoceratops* came a family of much larger dinosaurs. Many had long bony frills that protected their backs, and most also grew

Four horned dinosaurs. *Protoceratops* or another small kind gave rise to giants like *Triceratops*.

Protoceratops   Monoclonius   Styracosaurus

Above: Triceratops snapped off foliage with its beak and sliced it with teeth that cut like scissors.

Triceratops

horns that jutted up above the eyes and nostrils.

Largest and most formidable of all horned dinosaurs was *Triceratops* ('three-horned face'). *Triceratops* measured 11 metres and weighed 8.5 tonnes. Of all dinosaurs only the sauropods were larger. When *Triceratops* put down its mighty head and charged even *Tyrannosaurus* probably ran away.

The Dinosaurs' World

This chapter is about living things that shared the dinosaurs' world. All dinosaurs depended on other living things. The largest dinosaurs ate plants. The big flesh-eating dinosaurs ate the plant-eaters. The smaller dinosaurs largely ate reptiles, birds, mammals, maybe even insects. Many plants and most creatures of the Age of Dinosaurs are now extinct, just like the dinosaurs themselves. But they fitted well into the world of their time.

That world was very different from ours. Before the dinosaurs appeared, all the continents had been joined in one great landmass. During the Age of Dinosaurs that mass of land was breaking up. But this happened so slowly that many dinosaurs and other land animals had time to spread to lands now separated by the oceans. Meanwhile those lands stayed hot. Even certain places now in chilly polar regions were then comfortably warm.

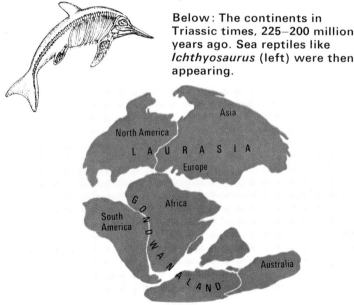

Below: The continents in Triassic times, 225–200 million years ago. Sea reptiles like *Ichthyosaurus* (left) were then appearing.

Continents were drifting apart through Jurassic times, 200–135 million years ago. Ammonites (left) flourished in the seas.

Below: The continents during Cretaceous times, 135–65 million years ago. The skeleton (left) is of an *Iguanodon*.

Prehistoric Plants

Dinosaurs spread far across the land, but only after land plants had got there first. For all dinosaurs depended in some way on land plants for their food.

If dinosaurs had appeared much sooner than they did, they would have had to live in swamps and on the banks of rivers. For early land plants grew only where the soil was wet. They sprang from tiny specks called spores that needed damp soil to protect them from drying out. By the time the Age of Dinosaurs began many swamps had dried up, but there were new plants able to live on dry land.

Plants from the Age of Dinosaurs. They included ginkgoes; swamp cypress; palm-like cycads and bennettitaleans; ferns; tree ferns and horsetails.

Naked Seeds

The new land plants produced large and small spores. The large spores stayed on the parent plants. The small spores blew away as pollen. A pollen grain that landed on a large spore fertilized it. The spore became a seed and fell to the ground. The seed's outer coat kept it moist until rain watered the soil. Then the seed began to sprout.

Trees that grew from such seeds included palm-like cycads and cone-bearing trees called conifers. Both have seeds only partly protected by an outer case. So these trees are known as *gymnosperms*, meaning 'naked seeds'. Gymnosperms thrived in the Age of Dinosaurs, and some kinds still survive.

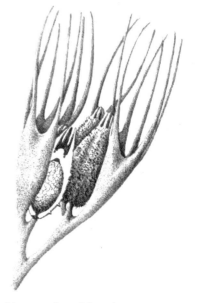

Above: the oldest known seed, from a plant that grew 390 million years ago. Its protective leafy bract differed from the woody cone of a modern conifer (below).

Capsule Seeds

The flowering plants arrived half-way through the Age of Dinosaurs. The flowers attracted insects that helped to spread their pollen. Their seeds were well protected by a fruit or capsule. So flowering plants are called *angiosperms*, meaning 'capsule seeds'.

As the Age of Dinosaurs ended, the flowering plants invaded the lands once covered by cycads and their kin.

49

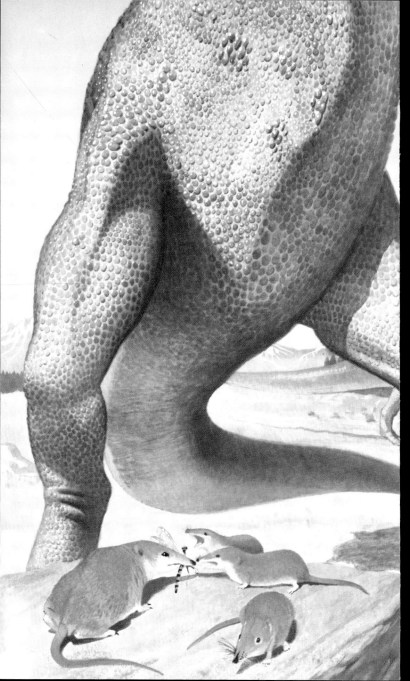

The First Mammals

Where dinosaurs walked, furry creatures scampered from their path. These tiny shrew-like beasts were the world's first mammals – warm-blooded forebears of the whale and elephant.

A family of early, tiny shrew-like mammals eats an insect, unnoticed by the dinosaur that towers above.

Mammals came from reptiles. Modern reptiles are cold-blooded: their temperature is the same as that of their surroundings. Reptiles are active only when the air is warm. Their skins have scales, not hair. Their teeth are all alike. Their legs are short and their knees and elbows tend to stick out at the sides.

Mammal-like Reptiles

When the Age of Dinosaurs began, unusual reptiles had appeared. Many had legs which stood below the body rather than at the side. They had some teeth shaped to cut and others shaped to chew. They may also have been warm-blooded, with hair to stop their body heat from leaking out.

Dinosaurs killed off the mammal-like reptiles, but not before one small kind had given rise to mammals.

Early mammals hunted insects. They probably laid eggs, but fed their babies with milk from special glands. They could control their body temperature, and so remain active in cold weather. But they were too small to fight dinosaurs.

Lizards and Snakes

When the Age of Dinosaurs was young, new kinds of reptile kept appearing. Most lived on the land. Some of these died out long ago. Others are alive today.

Gliding Lizards

Lizards are among the oldest living groups of reptiles. Some of the earliest known kinds of lizard were surprisingly like gliding lizards alive today. These lizards have long ribs covered with a flap of skin. The creatures live high among the trees. When they leap into the air they spread their ribs and the flap of skin on each side of the body acts like a parachute. The lizards can glide up to 13 metres without losing much height.

The prehistoric lizard *Kuehneosaurus* probably glided in the same way. The picture on the opposite page shows a gliding *Kuehneosaurus* with its skin flaps stretched.

Lizard Oddities

Lizards gave rise to some other reptiles. One was the strange, long-necked beast called *Tanystropheus*. There was also a group of large swimming 'lizards' known as mosasaurs. But most early lizards were small, shy insect-eaters like most lizards nowadays. They hid themselves when dinosaurs came by. The small flesh-eating dinosaurs no doubt killed and ate them if they could.

Tanystropheus was a strange, long-necked lizard. Almost all of its 6-metre long body was neck and tail. Over 200 million years ago it lived by the sea and ate fish, probably seizing them with sudden lunging movements of its neck.

The First Snakes

Lizards gave rise to snakes only as the Age of Dinosaurs was ending. These legless reptiles looked much like modern pythons – powerful snakes that coil around their prey and suffocate it.

Pythons and their relatives the boas have small spurs – reminders of the hind legs of their four-legged lizard ancestors.

Beak-heads

Among all living reptiles none is stranger than the tuatara from New Zealand. This creature looks like a lizard. In fact it is the only beak-head still alive.

Beak-heads had a beak-like upper jaw. The so-called rhynchosaurs were beak-heads 2 metres long. Flat plates inside their massive jaws helped to crush shell-fish or nuts. As dinosaurs grew plentiful, rhynchosaurs died out.

Wings of Skin

From the same group of reptiles that led to dinosaurs came creatures that were masters of the air. These creatures were the pterosaurs. Their name means 'winged lizards' and they came from gliding reptiles that must have looked much like the gliding lizards already mentioned.

Flimsy Gliders
By 200 million years ago many kinds of pterosaur were developing. All had a skeleton of thin, hollow, lightweight bones. Each skin wing was fixed to the long bones of an arm and a fourth finger. Both wings curved back to the hind legs.

Many pterosaurs had muscles that were too weak to flap their wings. So they simply glided on rising currents of warm air. But they steered well. By swooping low, they could have seized fishes or lizards in their long, beak-shaped jaws.

Pterosaurs were clumsy on land because their legs were very short. They could only shuffle along or hang upside down to sleep. But they slept on cliffs or treetops, safe from enemies.

Prow-beaks
Two main groups of pterosaurs evolved. The first of these is called ramphorhynchoids or 'prow-beaks'. Prow-beaks steered with long tails like rudders. Sharp teeth filled their beak-shaped jaws. The prow-beaks had rather short, broad wings and may have had the muscle power to flap them.

Remains of one prow-beak named 'hairy devil' had a covering of fur. Perhaps all pterosaurs were furry. Some experts think they must have been warm-blooded, too, if they had the energy to fly instead of simply gliding. If so, pterosaurs were not cold-blooded reptiles.

The second group of pterosaurs were pterodactyloids.

Left: *Dimorphodon* was an early pterosaur. It had a big skull and jaws armed with sharp teeth.

Below: *Pteranodon* drops fish from a mouth pouch to its young. It fished as it skimmed the sea, using its crest as a rudder to help it steer.

Winged Fingers

Pterodactyloid means 'winged fingers'. Most had long wings, little or no tail and a toothless beak.

Some were as small as a sparrow. Others were bigger than an eagle. *Pteranodon* was a glider with a wingspan of 7 metres. But *Quetzalcoatlus* had a wingspan twice as great as that. No one knows how a beast that big got into the air.

The First Birds

Pterosaurs were not the only creatures taking to the air. The first birds flew 150 million years ago. Birds came from the same group of reptiles as the dinosaurs. In fact they may have come from *Compsognathus*. This was a hen-sized dinosaur related to the much larger ostrich dinosaurs.

Compsognathus looked very like a bird without wings. It could run quickly on its long hind legs. Its arms ended in three, clawed fingers. Its mouth held sharp teeth.

Keeping Warm

Small speedy *Compsognathus* used up energy so fast that it may have been warm-blooded. Otherwise it would have had to stop and rest often as ordinary reptiles do. Its body surface was large for its size, so *Compsognathus* would have cooled down quickly unless it could trap heat inside its body.

Creatures like *Compsognathus* may have trapped heat by means of the scales covering their bodies. Probably these scales split and the split ends meshed together, holding warm air against

the skin. Such scales were the first true feathers.

Ancient Wing

The earliest creature that was certainly a bird was *Archaeopteryx*, whose name means 'ancient wing'. In many ways *Archaeopteryx* looked much like a little dinosaur. Its mouth held teeth. Its tail was long and bony. Its arms had three fingers with claws. But there were three important differences: a backward pointing toe for perching; a backward pointing hip girdle bone; and feathered wings.

Three *Archaeopteryx* at a lagoon. One has fallen in the mud. The remains of such birds, now changed to stone, have turned up in southern West Germany.

How the First Birds Flew

Some people think *Archaeopteryx* spread its wings like nets to help it capture prey. Later it may have learned to fly by leaping off the ground. But most experts think the first birds clawed their way up tree trunks, and simply used their wings for gliding down again.

Archaeopteryx's feathered wings could survive damage that would have crippled a pterosaur's fragile skin wings. *Archaeopteryx* probably could not flap its wings hard enough to launch itself into flight. But birds could fly strongly before the Age of Dinosaurs ended.

Crocodiles and Turtles

Among the oldest groups of living reptiles are the crocodiles and turtles. Both date back more than 200 million years. While some of their relatives took to the air, crocodiles and many turtles led a life in water.

Crocodiles are the only living members of the so-called ruling reptiles, the group in which most people also place the dinosaurs. Like most modern crocodiles, those living in the Age of Dinosaurs lurked in pools and rivers. They swam well, and ran quite quickly on the land. But they liked to lie in ambush in the water, seizing animals that came down for a drink. Even quite large dinosaurs may have fallen victim to the giant crocodile *Deinosuchus*, which flourished about 75 million years ago. *Deinosuchus* measured 15 metres and its head alone was longer than the body of a man of ordinary height.

Tank-like Turtles

The first tortoises lived on land. Like tortoises today, they were protected by a heavy shell. Later on, some gave rise to turtles with a lighter, flatter shell and feet shaped as flippers. Some swam in pools and rivers. Others lived in the sea and only climbed ashore to lay their eggs. The great sea turtle *Archelon* measured 4 metres and lived about the same time as *Deinosuchus*, the largest-ever crocodile. Turtles and crocodiles have altered little since those times.

Top: *Proganochelys* was a tortoise that stomped around in Europe about 210 million years ago. Like land tortoises of today its body was guarded by a heavy shell.

Above: *Protosuchus* may have given rise to modern crocodiles though it had long legs and was more active.

Rutiodon was one of the phytosaurs or 'plant lizards'. The name is misleading. Phytosaurs used their sharp teeth to eat other animals, not the leaves of plants.

Fish Lizards

While dinosaurs ruled the land, big, streamlined reptiles were masters of the ocean. There were several kinds.

Early in the Age of Dinosaurs the most abundant were the nothosaurs. They looked rather like big lizards, but had flattened tails to help them swim. Some measured 6 metres. While nothosaurs used their sharp teeth to snap up fish, placodonts were eating shellfish on the sea bed. Placodonts looked rather like stubby nothosaurs. But they had peg-like front teeth for grasping shellfish, and flat back teeth to grind them up. Nothosaurs and placodonts would have come ashore to lay eggs or have babies.

Ichthyosaurs swam fast enough to catch fish. They also ate ammonites: relatives of the octopus but with a coiled shell. One kind of ichthyosaur had teeth designed for crushing shellfish.

Speedy Swimmers

The fastest reptiles in the prehistoric ocean were the ichthyosaurs, whose name means 'fish lizards'. These animals grew up to 10 metres long and they had streamlined bodies like those of modern dolphins. An ichthyosaur swam by bending its back and thrusting water backwards with its fish-like tail. A tall fin on its back helped it to keep its balance, and it steered and braked with limbs that had evolved into flippers.

Ichthyosaurs had slender snouts and sharp teeth with which they crunched up prey.

A Mysterious Past

Ichthyosaurs came from some kind of land-living reptile. But we do not know which one. The remains of the oldest-known ichthyosaur show a creature with a long, slim tail instead of a 'fish' tail like the later ichthyosaurs. But even that animal was so well designed for water life that it could not have moved if stranded on dry land.

Unlike most reptiles now alive, ichthyosaurs were born in water, not hatched or born on the land. Newborn babies had to swim up quickly to breathe air.

Plesiosaurs

The nothosaurs mentioned on page 60 died out early in the Age of Dinosaurs. But they gave rise to a long-lasting group of swimming reptiles. These were the plesiosaurs, whose name means 'near lizards'.

These big sea reptiles had broader bodies than the nothosaurs. Their tails were short and not much use for swimming. Plesiosaurs rowed along, using their broad flat flippers as oars. They steered to one side by pushing one 'oar' forwards and pulling another backwards.

Some plesiosaurs had long necks, others short necks.

Long-necked Plesiosaurs
Someone wrote that these strange reptiles looked like a snake threaded through a turtle. They had short flippers but a long, thin neck and a small head. A long-necked plesiosaur would have swum on the surface, with its head above water. When it saw a fish, its head stabbed down on its prey.

These reptiles could not lift their flippers higher than their hips and shoulders. This meant that they were unable to dive.

The Pliosaurs
Short-necked plesiosaurs are called pliosaurs. These creatures had a short neck, long flippers and a large head with powerful jaws. They could swim faster and farther than their long-necked relatives, and they could dive to hunt for food.

Pliosaurs largely hunted relatives of the octopus. But *Kronosaurus* may even have hunted long-necked plesiosaurs. This pliosaur was 17 metres long and its head was longer than two men lying end to end.

A small pliosaur fishes as a large plesiosaur rears above a flying pterosaur.

A small pliosaur

Elasmosaurus

Rhamphorhynchus

After the Dinosaurs

Dinosaurs thrived for a much longer period than man has lived on Earth. They died out long before the first man appeared. So did pterosaurs and the big sea reptiles.

About 65 million years ago dinosaurs like those shown here were plentiful. They perished suddenly and the reason is a mystery.

Tyrannosaurus

Triceratops

Euoplocephalus

Parasaurolophus

Ornithomimus

Killed by Suicide?

Just what was it that killed off the dinosaurs so many years ago?

Some people think the dinosaurs themselves were to blame. One idea is that the flesh-eaters killed all the rest and then starved to death. Another is that the last dinosaurs were so strangely shaped that they could not breed.

Killed by Enemies?

Others argue that the dinosaurs were killed by enemies. Perhaps small mammals ate their eggs. Or germs may have brought disease that wiped them out. Plants may have produced poisons which killed the dinosaurs that ate them.

Killed by Cold?

Some people blame changes to the world the dinosaurs inhabited. Perhaps they were drowned by floods, poisoned by volcanic gases or killed by deadly rays from a far-off exploding star.

The guess most likely to be right is that they died of cold. The world was cooling down when they vanished. Even if they were warm-blooded they lacked hair to trap body heat and they were too big to burrow to escape the frosts of winter.

The Rise of the Birds

Warm-blooded animals with fur or feathers could keep warm even in cold weather. So the drop in temperature that may have killed off the dinosaurs did not wipe out the birds or mammals. Indeed, life was easier without the big dinosaurs to hunt them down.

New kinds of bird had been appearing even while the dinosaurs still ruled the land. From *Archaeopteryx* (above) came birds that lived on coasts and hunted fish. Like *Archaeopteryx*, they still had teeth.

Wingless Wonders

After the dinosaurs and big sea reptiles died out, many birds lost the need to fly away from enemies. From such birds came many flightless kinds. Giant penguins and giant flightless pelicans hunted fish in the seas. Flightless birds taller than a man and armed with savage beaks and claws lived on land. Like the flesh-eating dinosaurs they probably ran down and killed other animals. Other giant, flightless birds took the place once held by browsing dinosaurs. Such birds included New Zealand's giant moa and Madagascar's elephant bird. They were like today's ostriches, but far bigger, and lived mainly by eating plants.

Left: The gull-like seabird *Ichthyornis* lived when pterosaurs still thrived. Birds ousted them because birds were better fliers, having big flight muscles and a jutting chest bone to support them. Birds' feathered wings had the strong support of arm and wrist bones while a pterosaur's skin wing depended largely on the bones of just one finger.

Right: *Diatryma* stood taller than a man. It lived in North America 50 million years ago, after the last of the dinosaurs died out. A powerful beak and sharp claws would have made *Diatryma* more than a match for most of the animals it met up with.

A creodont about to attack. Creodonts were flesh-eating mammals killed off by later carnivores.

The Rise of Mammals

In the Age of Dinosaurs mammals were small and shy. After the dinosaurs, bigger, bolder kinds appeared. Some were fierce flesh-eaters. Others browsed or grazed peacefully on plants.

Mammals on the March

One early group of mammals gave rise to those strange egg-laying mammals the platypus and the echidna. Another group led to pouched mammals, or *marsupials*. Marsupials such as kangaroos give birth to tiny undeveloped babies. Most then grow in a pouch in the mother's belly. The second mammal group also gave rise to placental mammals like cats and sheep. These bear well-developed babies that have been nourished inside their mother's body by an organ called a *placenta*.

Each group of mammals competed for a living with the rest, and with the birds and reptiles. The placentals won. Today, these fill the places held 65 million years ago by flesh-eating and plant-eating dinosaurs.

Big cats became the most ferocious hunters of them all.

Below: These hoofed, plant-eating mammals lived in North America in prehistoric times. *Archaeotherium* (left) was a hog-like beast of 30 million years ago. Horse-like *Moropus* (middle) and deer-like *Synthetoceras* were both living at the same time, about 15 million years ago.

Four pictures show the story of a dinosaur that turned into a fossil. Left: A *Corythosaurus* (a duck-billed dinosaur) sinks, dying, in shallow water. Below: Mud covers the skeleton and delays decay. Minerals replace the bones as they rot.

Dinosaurs Preserved

Today mammals walk about on lands once ruled by dinosaurs. But though the dinosaurs are dead, they have not disappeared completely. The remains of many of them lie in the very rocks beneath the mammals' feet.

Everything we know about dinosaurs and how they lived comes from such remains, called *fossils*.

Fossil Mysteries

People have been finding fossil plants and creatures in the rocks for several thousand years. Until two centuries ago most people had no idea how fossils got there. Some thought that fossil sea shells had been washed up on the land by the great

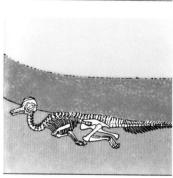

flood mentioned in the Bible. Two centuries ago, James Hutton showed that fossils were buried in the rocks while the rocks themselves were being made.

A Seabed Cemetery

Only a few of the countless millions of plants and animals that die form fossils. The rest decay or are eaten by scavenging animals.

Those most likely to be fossilized are the ones that sink to the bottom of a sea or lake where mud or sand covers and protects them.

Dinosaurs Under Water

But sometimes, a dinosaur would be drowned by river floods or fall into the sea. Under water its soft parts usually decayed before its body was covered up by the mud and sand that settled around it. But, sometimes mud settled fast enough to cloak the bones and guard these from decay.

Hard objects like bones, teeth, shells and branches are those most likely to be fossilized. But this process tends to change the objects' ingredients.

Fossils in the Making

As mud piled up around a seabed dinosaur, the weight of mud above squashed the mud around the skeleton and turned that mud to rock.

Meanwhile water had begun to dissolve the bones. But minerals seeping down with the water may have gradually filled the gaps left by the disappearing bone. In time, perhaps, hard mineral substances like silica or calcite entirely took the place of bone, so that the bone was turned to stone or *petrified*. Many dinosaur fossils formed like this.

Much later, movements of the Earth's crust may have raised the rocks around a fossil above the sea. As weather wore away the rocks above, the fossil bones were brought to the surface. Unless people save fossils these too are then worn away.

Above: The mud that lies around the dinosaur fossil has turned to rock. Movements of the Earth's crust have raised the rock as part of a mountain range. Right: Weather has worn away the rock and exposed the fossil dinosaur.

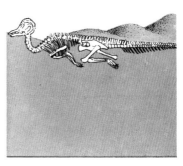

Discovering Dinosaurs

Hunting fossil dinosaurs can be difficult detective work. The main clues are of course the rocks that were being formed from materials like mud and sand while dinosaurs were still alive. These rocks show up on the surface only in certain areas. There, the places most worth searching are those where rain has stripped off surface soil and bared the rocks beneath.

Expert fossil hunters walk slowly over these rocks. They particularly look in gullies and below cliffs. Here, they examine fallen rocks and lumps of stone washed downhill by floodwater. For among the rocks and stones they may find small pieces broken from whole fossil skeletons still embedded in the rocks above.

Digging for Fossils

Even if he finds a fossil dinosaur embedded in the rock, a fossil hunter has only just begun his work. His next job is to get it out.

This could be impossible. The fossil may be half-way up a cliff. Or perhaps most of it has fallen out and been washed away.

Sometimes enough of a fossil dinosaur remains to make it worth excavating.

A whole team of people will be needed to free a set of giant fossil bones embedded in the rock. To reach the skeleton they may have to blow up or bulldoze many tonnes of rock.

Next they use picks and shovels to attack the rock around the bones. When they reach the bones they chip, scrape, and brush away the rock more carefully, using tools like chisels, trowels and stiff brushes.

Before they free the bones from the rock, the workers photograph and number them. Later this may help museum experts fit the bones together as they used to be.

Protecting Fossils

Freeing the bones of a large dinosaur may mean cutting each big bone into a number of pieces. Each piece must be protected for its journey to a museum. Fossil hunters paint the bones with a protective varnish. Next they add layers of paper. Then comes sacking, coated with plaster of Paris that sets hard. Thick wooden splints protect the whole package.

This fossil hunter uses a brush, trowel, chisel, hammer, spade and pick. They help her remove the rocks in which a fossil *Iguanodon* lies buried.

Rebuilding Dinosaurs

After a fossil dinosaur reaches a museum many months may pass before its skeleton is ready to be put on show.

The fossil bones may still be stuck in chunks of rock. Technicians first soak off the sack and paper bandages. Then they chip away the stone around the bones.

They may use several kinds of powered tools to help speed up their work. One tool that vibrates many thousand times a second works like a dentist's drill. Another tool uses sand particles in a jet of air to blast rock away from the fossil bone.

Studying the Bones

Once the fossil bones are cleaned and separated, experts need time to study them to work out how they joined together when their owner was alive.

This can be quite difficult, even if the bones were photographed just as they lay before the fossil hunters dug them out. Perhaps a carnosaur had pulled some bones apart just after the dinosaur had died. Or floodwater may have jumbled the bones into a heap before they hardened into fossils.

Building Up the Body

When the experts have solved the jigsaw puzzle of the bones, technicians can start to fit the bones together. Using metal rods and clamps to join the bones, they can rebuild the creature's skeleton and fix it upright as its owner used to stand.

Marks that show where muscles once joined bones help experts to work out the shape and size of the body. They can only guess its colour. Probably most dinosaurs were coloured to hide them from their enemies, as many mammals are today.

How they Lived

By studying fossil dinosaurs scientists can learn not only what the creatures looked like but how they lived. Leg bones show how a dinosaur walked. Its teeth tell us if it ate leaves or flesh. Holes in the skull are clues to the creature's type of brain, eyes, nose and ears. Once he knows what these were like, an expert can work out how well the creature thought, saw, smelt and heard. But there are still some puzzles.

Cold-Blooded or Warm?

Bone studies have shown that dinosaurs had a better blood supply than the cold-blooded reptiles. Yet experts used to say dinosaurs *were* reptiles. Some now argue that they were warm-blooded and unlike any other creatures. Much as we now know about them, these giants of the past are still mysterious.

Rebuilt skeleton of an Iguanodon

Surprising Facts

Giants and Dwarfs

Most dinosaurs were giants but some were smaller than a human. (*Compsognathus* was no larger than a hen.) This picture compares sizes of five dinosaurs, a pterosaur, a car and a man.

Heavy and Light

Of those creatures shown, easily the heaviest was *Brachiosaurus*. At up to 100 tonnes this monster weighed more than 1400 average men.

Next came *Apatosaurus* (also called *Brontosaurus*). This sauropod reached 30 tonnes —as much as 428 men. It would have taken three *Tyrannosauruses* to balance the weight of one *Apatosaurus*. At 8.5 tonnes, *Triceratops* was lighter than *Tyrannosaurus,* but heavier than an elephant. *Stegoceras* was much lighter still. Four *Pteranodons* weighed only as much as one man.

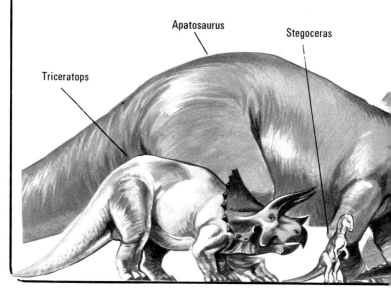

Triceratops

Apatosaurus

Stegoceras

Pteranodon

Brachiosaurus

Tyrannosaurus

Boneyard Bonanzas

Rich or unexpected finds of fossils have thrown new light on dinosaurs.

The Lost Herd
In 1878 a group of Belgian coal miners tunnelling underground found a whole fossil herd of *Iguanodons*. About 100 million years ago the beasts had fallen into a ravine that later filled with mud.

Workers brought up no fewer than 31 fossil *Iguano-* *dons*. Studying the remains gave experts their first true notion of what these dinosaurs had looked like.

A Missing Link
In 1969 a scientist collecting fossils on a cold Antarctic mountain found the remains of a *Lystrosaurus,* the sheep-sized reptile shown below.

Scientists knew this land animal had lived more than 200 million years ago in

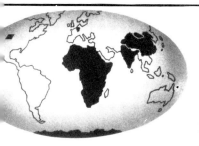

Above: Areas in black show fossil finds around the world.

Africa, India and China. It could have spread across these regions by walking. But it could not have swum across the sea to Antarctica. Finding *Lystrosaurus* fossils there helped to prove that some continents that are now far apart had been joined together when the Age of Dinosaurs was young.

Forgotten Fights

A few fossil finds show where one dinosaur attacked or ate another. The American Museum has a brontosaur skeleton whose tail bears *Allosaurus* teeth marks. Some *Allosaurus* teeth found near the fossil tail must have broken off when the hunter bit into its victim's tail bones.

In 1971 fossil hunters in Mongolia found the fossils of two dinosaurs that had died locked in combat. The flesh-eater *Velociraptor* had perished with its arms and legs grasping the head of a *Protoceratops,* one of the early horned dinosaurs.

Bones by the Truckload

Fossil hunters found huge numbers of fossil dinosaurs in certain rock formations. At Como Bluff, Wyoming, dinosaur bones were thickly strewn in rocks in a stretch of land 11 kilometres long.

Fossil Tracks and Traces

Their bones are not the only clues we have to the lives of creatures living in the Age of Dinosaurs.

We can learn much about them from other fossils, including fossils of their eggs, their footprints, droppings, and even remains of the meals they ate.

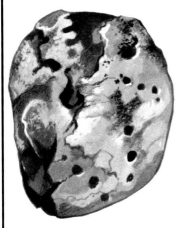

Human footprints to same scale

A Mosasaur's Meal

Tooth marks on the fossil ammonite above show it was bitten 16 times by a young mosasaur, a giant sea lizard. Such finds show how these prehistoric reptiles lived.

Giant Footprints

Sometimes dinosaurs left footprints in wet mud that dried and hardened into rock. The fossil footprints in this rock can tell us much about the creatures that made them scores of millions of years ago. For example, we discover that sauropods had feet as large as big bass drums.

One set of sauropod footprints showed the front feet only. Experts realized this meant the creature had been swimming, with its hind feet off the bottom.

At Glen Rose in Texas, fossil hunters unearthed tracks left by a sauropod and a flesh-eating dinosaur that had been chasing it. As workers removed the soft rock hiding the tracks they hoped to learn how the chase ended. Tantalizingly, the tracks vanished below a wall of rock too hard to remove.

Ancient Eggs

In the 1920s, an American called Roy Chapman Andrews led a number of expeditions to Mongolian deserts in search of fossils. Their most exciting finds were nests of eggs like those shown here. Some eggs had been smashed. Others held fossils of babies that had died before hatching. The eggs were those of the dinosaur *Protoceratops*.

In 1961 in France, fossil hunters found 80-million-year-old sauropod eggs twice as large as those laid by a modern ostrich. No known eggs of any kind are larger.

Freak Fossils

Not all prehistoric animals were turned to fossils by minerals that gradually took the place of their bones. Some fossils are simply hollows left in the rock when the bones dissolved away.

Other fossils are preserved because they were surrounded by substances like amber, ice, peat and tar.

Frozen Mammoths

Mammoths like the one shown on the left died out many thousand years ago. Many were buried under landslides of frozen soil that never melted. Some have been so well preserved by the cold that hair and even flesh survive.

In the last 250 years, people have found buried remains of 117,000 mammoths in Siberia, as well as others in North America and Europe. Ice Age rhinoceroses have also been found.

Tar Traps

Part of the Californian city of Los Angeles stands close to natural pools of tar. About 15,000 years ago wild beasts tried to drink the rainwater lying on the tar. But many creatures sank into the sticky pools and died. People digging up the now hardened tar deposits have found the bones of bison, horses, groundsloths, and mammoths. There are also remains of more than 1500 dire-wolves and 1000 sabre-toothed cats.

Famous Fossil Hunters

Much of what we know about the Age of Dinosaurs we owe to the fossil hunters of the 1800s. These pages tell of four important pioneers and the fossils they discovered.

Mary Anning

Mary Anning
Mary Anning (1799–1847) lived in Lyme Regis, a town in southern England. In nearby sea cliffs she unearthed many fossils dating from the Age of Dinosaurs. At the age of 11, she found the first full ichthyosaur skeleton. Later she found the first complete plesiosaur fossil and the first British pterodactyl fossil.

Gideon Mantell
Dr Mantell (1790–1852) was an English country doctor who began the age of dinosaur discovery. In 1822 his wife saw fossil teeth embedded in a roadside rock. They reminded Gideon of an iguana lizard's. He named their prehistoric owner *Iguanodon* ('iguana tooth') and published his idea of *Iguanodon*'s appearance.

In 1841 a British scientist invented the name dinosaurs (meaning 'terrible lizards') for *Iguanodon* and giant creatures like it.

Gideon Mantell

Othniel Marsh

Edward Drinker Cope

Edward Drinker Cope (1840–1897) was an American naturalist who studied extinct backboned animals of western North America. He and Marsh were rivals. Each tried to find more prehistoric creatures than the other.

In the late 1870s teams of fossil hunters hired by Cope and Marsh spied on one another and once actually came to blows.

Cope and his workers found nine new genera of fossil dinosaur. Cope spent all his money and died poor. But most of his dinosaurs are still treasured in a New York natural history museum.

Edward Drinker Cope

Othniel Marsh

Othniel Marsh (1831–1899) was an American *palaeontologist* (a scientist who studies fossils). In 1866 he became professor at a natural history museum founded at Yale College by his own uncle. For about 30 years Marsh sent teams of fossil hunters searching the United States for the remains of dinosaurs and other beasts.

Tonnes of fossil bones were shipped to Yale from western states. Marsh broke all records for numbers of new kinds of fossil dinosaurs discovered. Altogether he collected or described 19 different genera.

Dinosaurs That Never Were

The great dinosaurs looked like no creature now alive. This made it difficult for the first discoverers of dinosaurs to judge exactly how their jumbled fossil bones had linked together. Not surprisingly some early bids to rebuild dinosaurs produced absurd mistakes.

Iguanodon had no horn on its snout, but a spiky thumb on each forelimb. Hawkins found only one fossil thumb, so thought it natural to put it on the monster's snout.

Mythical Monsters

The strange scene on the left shows a sculptor's London workshop in 1835. Benjamin Waterhouse Hawkins was making life-size models of prehistoric beasts to decorate a park at Sydenham. Some of his monsters still stand there today.

Hawkins had little notion of the beasts' true shapes or sizes. His *Iguanodon* (the middle animal) appeared as a giant, four-legged rhinoceros. In fact *Iguanodon* was a two-legged dinosaur without a horn, as shown above.

Hawkins also wrongly showed an early amphibian (left) and reptile (right) as a frog and a tortoise.

Heads or Tails?

In 1868 American fossil hunters working for Edward Drinker Cope discovered the fossil of a long-necked swimming reptile. Cope named the plesiosaur *Elasmosaurus*, meaning 'ribbon reptile'. He proudly described it as unlike any other reptile.

People marvelled at the strange shape of the rebuilt skeleton in the Academy Museum at Philadelphia. But Professor Joseph Leidy saw that something was wrong. He took away the last 'tail' bone and showed that it should join on to the head.

Cope's reptile was unique because he had simply stuck the head on the wrong end.

Dinosaurs in the News

More than one and a half centuries have passed since people first found fossil dinosaurs. But new finds keep being made and are still adding to our knowledge of those vanished giants.

Here are a few of the more important dinosaur discoveries made in various places since the middle 1970s.

Dinosaur Family Life

Experts argue whether dinosaurs cared for their young or simply laid eggs and walked away.

In 1979 American fossil hunters working in Montana found hints that at least some dinosaurs stayed around to help their babies.

The main clue was a dip in the ground. This nest held fossil skeletons of eleven baby duck-billed dinosaurs, each about one metre long. They were plainly hatchlings, for some of their bones had not yet hardened. Yet their teeth showed signs of wear. This showed that the parents had probably brought food to their youngsters before they were old enough to leave the nest to find food for themselves.

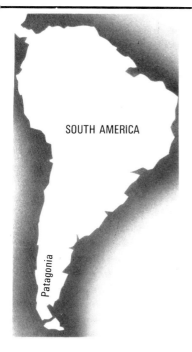

SOUTH AMERICA

Patagonia

Finds from Patagonia

In 1979 scientists announced finds of 'new' fossil dinosaurs discovered in Patagonia in southern Argentina.

Piatwitzkysaurus was a flesh-eater nearly four metres high, with teeth like daggers. *Patagosaurus* and *Volkheimeria* were big plant-eating sauropods. All of these dinosaurs lived more than 135 million years ago.

Differences between such dinosaurs and those in North America help to show how various dinosaurs evolved.

Savage Swimmers

In 1980 there came proof that the two-legged flesh-eating dinosaurs could swim. The proof was a group of fossil tracks in the dried bed of a prehistoric lake in the American state of Connecticut.

One track showed that the claw and tip of each middle toe had hit bottom first, then outer claws had scraped backwards as the creature kicked through deep water over 150 million years ago.

Living Fossils

Few kinds of creature live more than a few million years. Those living in the Age of Dinosaurs have mostly gone. Yet some species have survived almost unaltered since those distant days.

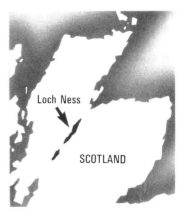

Loch Ness

SCOTLAND

Lake Monsters

Travellers' tales and legends suggest that plesiosaurs still live in deep and lonely lakes. The best known of these supposed survivors from the ancient past is the Loch Ness monster. Many people say they have seen strange humps or a long neck rise above the Scottish lake from which the monster gets its name. But no dead or living plesiosaur has been caught to prove that such a creature is really there.

Coelacanth

The King Crab

This horseshoe-shaped sea creature is not in fact a crab. King crabs are the only living relatives of trilobites—animals that died out as much as 250 million years ago.

A Fishy Surprise

Coelacanths were lobe-finned fishes thought to have died out 70 million years ago. But in 1938 a trawler hauled up a living specimen off South Africa. Since then many have been captured.

INDEX

Page numbers in *italics* refer to illustrations.